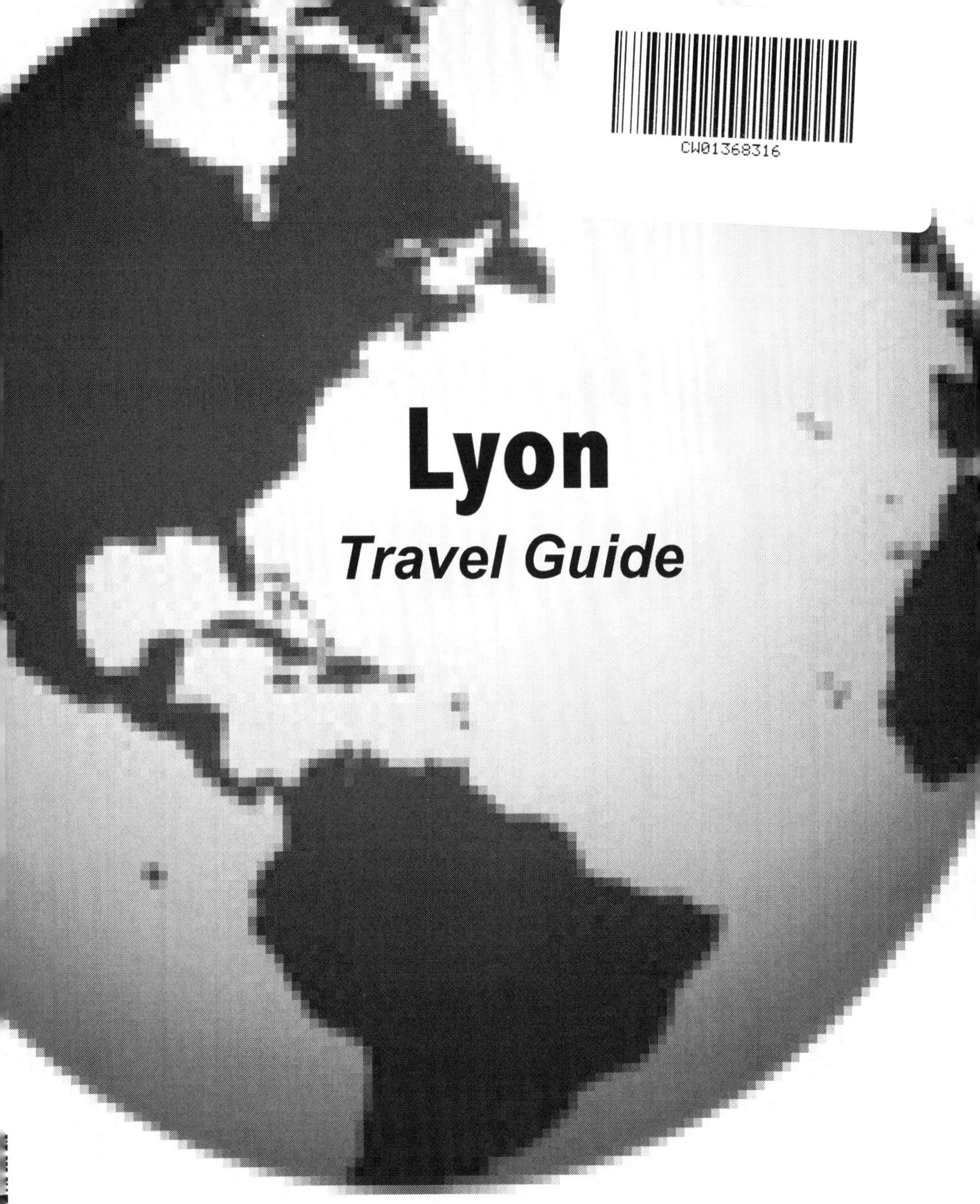

Lyon

Travel Guide

Quick Trips Series

Table of Contents

Lyon

Located at the confluence of the Rhône and Saone rivers, Lyon is one of the largest cities in France and is an important French business and cultural centre. The city has noted historical sights like the Roman City and the Notre-Dame de Fourviere Cathedral. 'Vieux Lyon' (Old Town) is a gourmand's delight and has many beautiful Renaissance houses.

Lyon is a gastronomic capital with delightful bistros where you can dine on specialties that have made Lyonnais cuisine famous all over the world. Diners can enjoy a glass of fine red wine from vineyards in the hills surrounding Lyon.

Lyon is known for its banking, pharmaceutical and biotech industries, as well as its intense cultural activity at a variety of museums, theatres and opera houses. Buy a Lyon City Card and be ready to cost-effectively explore the monuments and sights of the city. The card gives free access to public transportation and free entrance to more than 25 museums.

Customs & Culture

Lyon is a city where the past combines nicely with the present to make a pleasant metropolis of manageable size despite the population of 2 million. The residents of the region speak several dialects of provincial French (a result of Lyon's Middle Ages inhabitants).

In the 16th century, Lyon became a centre for the printing of books and it attracted many poets from all over Europe. Later it was known for its Cinema of Lights and the Museum of Lights can still be visited today. The city hosts the Festival of Lights, every year on 8th December, when every house in the city will have candles on their windows, creating a spectacular illuminated view.

The National Orchestra and the Auditorium offer performances regularly. Visit a performance at the

Subsistence Complex which employs artists in theater, modern circus and dance. It focuses on young, local talent including students at the University of Lumière in Lyon. Lyon has a long history of craftsmen specialising in silk production (visit the Croix - Rousse district to see them in action) and Lyon was historically a major silk trading city.

Geography

Lyon is located in the East-Central part of France between Paris and Marseille in the Rhône-Alpes region. The Rhône and Saone rivers converge near the historic centre of the town, forming a peninsula. On the west and north, the city is dominated by two large hills, Fourvière and Croix - Rousse, where the Old City is located (a UNESCO World Heritage site). At the east of Rhône is the modern city of Lyon where the majority of the population lives and the location of the business district and much of the city's economic activity.

The Saint Exupéry Airport is located 20 km southeast of the center and you can travel from there to all over the city. Part-Dieu railway station, situated on the Paris-Lyon-Marseille line can be reached by metro, tram and the Rhônexpress.

The city is divided into 9 districts and transportation is available by car, taxi, funicular, tramways, bus, metro and bike. There are a lot of discounts for transportation and one of them in the City Card (available for 1, 2 or 3 days.) This will give you free access to public transportation and more.

To purchase a City Card visit: http://www.en.lyon-france.com/Lyon-City-Card/Order-your-Lyon-City-Card

More information and a map of the city is here: http://www.ccc-lyon.com/coming-in-lyon/google-map-earth/google-earth

To see today's weather in Lyon visit: http://www.worldweatheronline.com/Lyon-weather/Rhone-Alpes/FR.aspx

Weather & Best Time to Visit

Lyon has a subtropical climate with dry and cold winters, averaging 3 °C (38 °F) in the month of January. Summers are warm, with an average temperature of 22 °C (71 °F) in July. The climate is similar to the rest of France, and with cultural activities planned throughout the year, you should visit Lyon in any season. Rainfall is moderate all year, averaging 830 millimeters (32.7 in).

Like all of France, summertime is the busiest and has the hottest weather. Fourvière Hill is beautiful in summertime when you can take a train through the hill to reach the Notre- Dame Cathedral.

Sights & Activities: What to See & Do

Notre-Dame de Fourviere

8 Place de Fourvière,

69005 Lyon

Tel: 04 78 25 13 01

http://www.fourviere.org/fr_FR/index.php

This place has long been a focal point of Lyon with much religious history taking place on Fourvière Hill. The basilica is positioned near the top of Fourvière hill and it incorporates a museum of religious art, and a treasury. Pilgrims from far and wide gather here to pay homage to the Virgin Mary. The Festival of Lights is also dedicated to her.

The Cathedral was built in 1870 and was dedicated to the Virgin Mary for saving the Lyonnais from a disease epidemic that plagued Europe in the 19th century.

The Neo-Byzantine cathedral has a lot in common with Sacre-Coeur Cathedral in Paris with both built in a similar architectural style and sharing a similar history. The interior of the church is impressive and when the church bells ring, it's like hearing a chime from heaven!

The museum of the church holds an important collection of religious items, both ancient and contemporary. You can rent an audio guide to learn about the rich religious history of Notre-Dame.

A guided tour of the church costs €2. Entry to the museum costs €5 and it is open daily from 8:00am to 7:00pm.

Old City

'The Old City of Lyon' is the historical, ancient part of the city of Lyon, and one of the largest Renaissance neighborhoods in Europe. The district covers 3 areas, each of them rich in history. Saint Georges was home to the silk workers in the 16th century and the architecture of the buildings has an industrial feel. This part features ancient roads that pass by the buildings and connect the streets.

Saint-Paul was popular with Italian bakers and today you can visit the Bullioud hotel and the Gadagne hotel, buildings strongly influenced by the Italian culture. The

Historical Museum of Lyon and the Puppet Museum are also points of interest here, as well as the Romanesque Church of Saint-Paul with its spectacular lantern tower.

Saint-Jean dates from the Middle Ages and it was the political and religious powerhouse of the city as well as the seat of the Primate of Gaul. The predominant style of architecture here is Gothic, with a few Romanesque buildings. Other highlights here are the Cathedral and the Museum of Miniatures & Film Sets.

Croix-Rousse District

The name of the district means 'russet cross' and comes from the Christians who erected a cross in the market here in the 16th century. The district is located on the Croix - Rousse hill near the Place des Terraux square. It is known as the 'working hill', because of the silk workers who moved here in the 18th century.

Silk workers from all over the world gathered and lived here having an important role and influence in the expansion of the city. The neighborhood was built to meet the daily demands of the workers and the architecture of the houses is simple with an basic touch. The district started to be redeveloped in the 18th century, after the silk workers revolted. Today you will find a lot of restaurants, bistros, gift shops as well as silk shops in the area.

Lyon River Cruises

13 Bis Quai Rambaud,

69002 Lyon

Tel: 04 78 42 96 81

http://www.lyoncityboat.com/

The Rhône and Saone rivers make their way through the city and offer pleasant water views as you move across the city. The city provides several guided boat tours. The Hermes Boat is the biggest luxury boat on the river and gives a French experience. You can enjoy the view and commentary while having a glass of local wine and tasting a few appetizers.

Don't miss a cruise after dark. At nighttime, the city is transformed: the architecture of the buildings and the lights throughout the city offer a spectacular view and it's an impressive and photogenic sight from the boat. The cost for a journey on the river varies but starts at just €7.

Lyon Business District

http://www.business.greaterlyon.com

In the past, Lyon was an important book-publishing center, a center for the silk industry and today is a city of gastronomical delights. Lyon is the second-most important economic city in France after Paris.

The business district is located in the Part - Dieu district and it is headquarters of French companies, including intergovernmental agencies and Euronews. Due to its geographic position between Paris and Marseille, Lyon is an ideal place for running a corporation.

Beside the companies, there are universities and research centers including The Light University of Lyon. Lyon is one of the leading cities in France for energy, IT and digital industries and an important medical research center. Take a walk around and admire the ultra-modern buildings here.

Bonaparte Bridge

The bridge crosses the riverbank to the Old Town and it has been compared with the Pont Neuf bridge in Paris because of the view that it reveals. Initially, the bridge was an access way for merchandisers and was built from wood between the years of 1634 and 1642 by Jean Christophe. It had suffered numerous floods and it was rebuilt several times and in 1807 it was redesigned in stone. In 1944, the bridge was destroyed by German Nazi bombing and the current bridge was rebuilt in 1950.

Contemporary Art Center

48 Quai Rambaud,

69001, Lyon

Tel: +33 (0) 4 27 82 69 40

http://www.lasucriere-lyon.com/

Combining the old history of the city with modernity, the contemporary art center had become one of the most visited art galleries in Lyon. 'The Sugar', as it is nicknamed, was originally built in the 1930s as a sugar factory. The building was abandoned, and in the year 2003 it was turned into an exhibition and event place. This large and magnificent structure covers four floors and holds private and public exhibitions and cultural events. Young artists are supported here to expose their work and to share their knowledge.

City Hall

The City Hall is an ornate building located in front of the Opera, near Place des Terraux. It was built by Simon Maupin, an architect that became famous after designing this building. This majestic building dates back from 1651 and in the year of 1674 it was restored after a fire. During the French Revolution the front part of the building was damaged.

Tete d'Or Park

1 Boulevard du 11 Novembre 1918,

69006 Lyon

Tel: +33 4 72 82 35 00

http://www.loisirs-parcdelatetedor.com/

The Park was opened in the year 1856 and covers 117 hectares. Conveniently located near the town center, it is accessible to everyone in central Lyon. The park is a great place to go with the entire family to visit the zoo, botanical gardens, lake shores and to sunbathe in the nice weather.

You can take your children on a pony ride here. The Zoo within the park has over 1,000 animals (300 bred in captivity and 700 wild animals). The animal trainers are happy to answer questions and often put on shows for the enjoyment of children.

The Botanical Garden is one of the biggest in Europe, having over 15,000 species of plants from all over the world. There are various greenhouses for the orchids and another for the tropical plants. Visit on foot or rent a bike or take the mini train that runs throughout the park on a guided tour. A 20 minute tour costs €4 for adults and €2 for children.

Silk Workers House (Maison des Canuts)

10 et 12 Rue d'Ivry, 69004, Lyon

Tel: 04 78 28 62 04

http://maisondescanuts.com/

The Silk Workers House is a tribute to the silk industry that left a mark all over the city. It is a UNESCO World Heritage site and it is located on the Croix - Rousse hill. Take a journey back in time by taking an informative tour and find out all about silk manufacturing and the tools used in the process.

Learn about the impact of the invention of Jacquard loom and the daily life of the silk workers. The house has a gift shop where you can buy silk products that are still made here using the same ancient techniques.

Water City (Rhone River Museum)

17, rue de la République,

69002 Lyon

http://www.lacitedeleau.fr/infos-pratiques.html

Water is vital for us all and the city of Lyon is surrounded by water. This is a fun place to learn about water and how to use it in a responsible way. The purpose of this project is to educate people about the problems of wasting water and ways to improve the usage of water. Children will have lots of fun here. Free admission.

Museums in Lyon

Because of his rich history, Lyon has a museum recording many aspects of its past. Most of the collections are meaningful, rare and have an educational purpose as well as testifying the history of the city and the numerous people that have lived here over the centuries.

Fine Arts Museum

20 Place des Terreaux, F-69001 Lyon

Tel: 33 (0)4.72.10.17.40

http://www.mba-lyon.fr

Located in the hearth of Lyon, near Place des Terraux Square, in a 17th Benedictine building, the Museum of Fine Arts has the second largest collection of drawings, sculptures, decorative arts and antiquities in Europe, after the Louvre in Paris.

The art is displayed in over 70 rooms on three floors. You can visit both permanent collections and temporary exhibitions. This museum has some unique displays, like the Egypt antiques including funerary practices, images of the Gods and The Pharaoh.

African Museum of Lyon

150, Cours Gambetta

69361 Lyon Cedex 07

Tel: 04 78 61 60 98

The African Museum of Lyon is one of the oldest museums in France as well as the oldest African museum in the country. Founded in the year 1863 by the African Missionary Society, the museum holds over 2,000 works about the religious, cultural and daily life of West Africa as well as the cultural meeting of Europe with Africa.

The museum also helps to promote contemporary artists from all over Africa with displays of their work. This includes photographers, sculptors and self-taught artists. The library within the museum is accessible to all, and has many documents, research files, books and journals about African culture. Visitors can also research using the computers provided by the museum.

Henri-Malartre Museum

645 Rue du Musée Rochetaillée

sur Saône

69270 Lyon

Tel: +33 4 78 22 18 80

http://www.musee-malartre.com

If you enjoy luxury cars and are passionate about vintage cars, this museum should be on your list of places to visit. Henry Malartre, a metal dealer started a private collection of motors and cars in 1931. Later on, he opened the Musee de l' Automobile Henri Malartre in a castle dating from the 15th century. In the year of 1972 the museum was bought by the Lyon City Council and altered to what you see today.

You can see over 150 cars, motorbikes, bicycles and other transportation from the first steam cars to modern cars like a Mclaren racing car. Some of the automobiles displayed in the museum are unique. There are also regular events and car shows in collaboration with brands like Rolls Royce. The cost of an adult ticket is €6. Children are not charged.

Gallo-Roman Civilization Museum

17 Rue Cleberg,

69005 Lyon

Tel: 04 72 38 81 90

The Gallo-Roman society on the hills of Fourvière was a powerful establishment as long ago as the late 1st century BC. You can still see the ruins of the ancient city as well as a lot of artifacts used in the religious and daily life of the Gallo-Romans. The museum is located on the Fourvière Hill, near the Roman theatre, and it was opened in 1975. The architecture of the building was designed by Bernard Zehrfuss and is quite unique. As you visit, you will descend down concrete stairs to visit the display rooms.

The Gallo-Roman Civilization museum holds a unique collection of Celtic, Roman and Pre-Roman artifacts, the ruins of the ancient town of Gaul as well as scale models of the major buildings, such as the Odeon. Most of the objects displayed here were discovered on the archeological site nearby, and the museum also hosts collections from other parts of Europe. The entry fee is €6.50 and it is open daily.

Modern Art Museum

81 Quai Charles-de-Gaulle,

Cité - Internationale,

69006, Lyon

Tel: 04 72 69 17 17

http://www.mac-lyon.com/mac/

Lyon also promotes modern art and contemporary culture

at places like the Modern Art Museum. Located in front of the Tete d'Or Park, the museum was opened in 1995 and was designed by Italian architect, Renzo Piano.

It has over 100 exhibitions by modern artists like Trisha Brown and Olivier Mosset. The building hosts a series of events dedicated to young artists, holds conferences and awards events. On the website you will find a list of upcoming events and exhibitions.

Budget Tips

 Accommodation

Hilton Hotel

70 Quai Charles de Gaulle,

69463, Lyon

Tel: 33-4-7817-5050

http://www3.hilton.com

Located near the Rhone River, with a view over the Tete D'or Park and only 5 minutes walk from Lyon's city center, this hotel is in the perfect location for the visitor to Lyon. The hotel offers parking, two restaurants and bar, fitness center and internet access. You can enjoy a beautiful view from the hotel. The prices for rooms are between €150 and €220/night with breakfast.

La Residence Hotel

18, Rue Victor Hugo,

69002, Lyon

Tel: 33 (0) 478 42 63 28

http://www.hotel-la-residence.com/

La Residence is a popular hotel in which to stay in Lyon and offers pleasant treatment of foreign language speakers. The hotel is located in the center of the city, near the Old Town. It has a modern architecture and a cozy interior, and staff here are delighted to help you navigate the city.

There are 67 rooms, all modern with soundproofing, TV, minibar and hairdryer. The restaurant of the hotel is recognized for the quality and freshness of the dishes and the bar has a good selection of special drinks including a good selection of wines from all over France. The cost for a double room is about €94 per night.

Hotel Berlioz

12 Cours Charlemagne,

69002, Lyon

Tel: +33 4 78 42 30 31

www.hotel-berlioz.com

Hotel Berlioz was built in 1965 and has had numerous renovations since then. The hotel is located just a few minutes walk from the Old City, the Croix - Rousse district and the Peninsula. You have easy access to the main highlights of Lyon as well to public transport. The rooms are equipped with LCD TVs, telephone, radio and internet access.

The restaurant and bar area offers a beautiful view over the garden of the hotel. Reception is opened 24x7 and it makes available a variety of services, such assistance with train reservations. This is a great location if you are looking for a quiet place to stay in Lyon. The cost for a room can vary between €77 and €130, depending on the season and type of room.

Radisson Blu Hotel

129 Rue Servient Lyon 3°

69003, Lyon

Tel: + 33 (4) 78635500

http://www.radissonblu.com/hotel-lyon

It large hotel is located in the Part - Dieu district on the east side of the Peninsula. You can easily reach public transportation: the tramway stops in front of the hotel and the subway station, the Rhonexpress and TGV are just 300 meters walk away.

It is a 4 star hotel and offers free Wi-Fi internet, late check-out, express laundry, express check-out and more. The breakfast is included in the price and it consists in an extensive buffet with European and American cuisine. The rooms give views of the city or the mountains. Rooms are equipped with mini-bar, air-conditioning, bathtub, high-speed internet and TV. You can also bring your pet. The price of a standard double room is €99.

Hotel des Celestins

4 Rue des Archers,

69002 Lyon

Tel: +33 4 72 56 08 98

http://www.hotelcelestins.com/

Hotel des Celestins is an ideal place to stay. Located in the heart of Lyon near the Old Town there is a panoramic view from many of the rooms. The hotel offers a range of services and has a restaurant, bar and parking for clients. The rooms are equipped with air-conditioning, internet access and TV. The price for a standard double room varies between €84 and €134, depending on the season.

Restaurants, Cafés & Bars

From the 19th century, Lyon was recognized as a world culinary capital when silk industry made famous little family-run businesses called ‘bouchons’. Today, you will still find a lot of little bistros. Look for traditionally made croissants and different varieties of chocolate like raw chocolate. Lyonnais people enjoy simple imgredients and menus typically include plenty of meat, salad, cheese and desserts. The city is the hometown of the world-famous chef, Paul Bocuse.

Bernachon

42, Cours Franklin Roosevelt

69006, Lyon

Tel: +33 04 78 24 37 98

http://bernachon.com/

When you are in Lyon, visit one of the oldest bistros in town. Bernachon is a traditional family-run business with a lot of history and with products known all over the world.

In 1953, Maurice Bernachon inherited this little bistro and turned it into a small chocolate factory, which is still here today.

Bernachon pays special attention to chocolate: they buy the raw cocoa beans and roast, grind and blend them in-house. The ingredients they use come from controlled agricultures in countries like Ghana and Madagascar and the entire process of making the chocolate is passed down within the family. Taste their famous President Cake or their 'Palet d'or' Cake for about €8 for 100 grams. You can also taste other affordable specialties like truffles, toffee and pralines.

Lyon Halls (Les Halles de Lyon)

102 Cours Lafayette, Lyon

Tel: 04 78 62 39 33

http://www.hallespaulbocuse.lyon.fr/

If you want to taste a variety of local specialties, visit the Lyon Halls, the biggest market in Lyon, located at the intersection of Garibaldi, Lafayette and Bonnel. It was opened in 1971 and has attracted local and national producers.

It is the place in Lyon where you can always find fresh and affordable products. With over 50 shops and restaurants, local bakers, butchers and vegetable stalls, this is the perfect place buy picnic items in Lyon. You can find most things here including seasonal fruits and vegetables, fresh meat, special cheeses, wines, chocolates. Look for flowers at 'The Palace of the Rose', an amazing flower shop with rare flowers.

Beside the restaurants and shops, you can find local growers on stalls with a variety of items from this region, including wines and cheeses made by people who live on the hills surrounding Lyon. The market opens at 7:00 in the morning at closes at 10:30 at night.

Clostan Catering

http://www.clostan.fr

This is a well-known restaurant inside the Lyon Halls and it stands out for the freshness and quality of the traditionally made products. You can buy local desserts like cheese cream and 'Baba Strawberry'. It has a store and a restaurant. The restaurant covers a large area and the interior is cozy. You can have a full menu for about €18, a cheese tray for about €8 and a bottle of local red wine for €10.

In Cuisine

1 Place Bellecour,

69002, Lyon

Tel: 04 72 41 18 00

http://www.incuisine.fr/en/index.html

If you are interested in the history of gastronomy in France you should visit 'In Cuisine,' a bookshop dedicated to food. Visit here to learn about world cooking, wines and nutrition. They also serve a nice lunch for €10 and coffee or tea for €1.50. This place, like some others in Lyon, was the subject of a BBC documentary about gastronomy.

The Georges Brewery

30 Cours de Verdun Perrache, Lyon

Tel: 04 72 56 54 54

http://www.brasseriegeorges.com/home.aspx

Located in the 2nd district of Lyon, The Georges Brewery is the oldest brewery in Lyon as well as one of the largest in France.

The Georges Brewery was opened in 1836 and it has had an historical part in the gastronomy culture of Lyon. The founder, Jean-Georges Hoffherr was an Alsatian brewer who studied the properties of the water in Lyon and decided to open the brewery here even though at that time, there were 26 other breweries in Lyon. He became famous for the quality of his beer and today the beer is still made from the same recipe.

The building has a stunning architectural design and among the years, many famous people come here including Jules Verne, Édith Piaf and Jacques Brel.

Nowadays the brewery has incorporated a restaurant, where you can have a traditional menu for about €30 per person.

Sushi Shop

11 Rue de la Barre, 69002, Lyon

Tel: +33 8 26 82 68 26

www.sushishop.fr

This Japanese restaurant will surprise you with the quality of the food, the variety of dishes and the cheap prices. If you are a vegetarian, you can choose from a wide assortment of rice and vegetables. They have lovely, fresh desserts, as well as some traditional Japanese dishes with ingredients like Shittake mushrooms and fried bamboo. Sushi is between €2 and €4 per item and a plate is between €10 and €20.

Café des Federations

8 Rue Major Martin, Lyon

Tel: +33 4 78 28 26 00

http://www.lesfedeslyon.com/

A traditional restaurant in Lyon, Café des Federations specialises in meat assortments such as pâtés and sausages. The place is often crowded and the restaurant is quite small but the interior is traditionally designed. Ask the staff for information about how the products have been prepared. A full meal will be around €40 for a good selection of small plates, desserts, cheese and wine.

Shopping

Lyonnais love shopping and the city has many shops, markets, specialized boutiques and commercial centers.

Commercial Center La Part-Dieu

17 Rue du Docteur Bouchut,

69003 Lyon

http://www.centrecommercial-partdieu.com/W/do/centre/accueil

The commercial center La Part-Dieu is one of the largest shopping malls in France based on the large number of stores. It has been in operation since 1975. The mall has five levels and an underground car park. It is located in the La Part-Dieu district. You can shop in 250 stores and dine in over 40 restaurants and snack bars.

Take a break and watch a 3D movie at one of the two cinemas, Stop and relax at one of rest areas inside the shopping mall. Famous brands from all over the world like Levis, Swatch, Fossil, Swarovski and more are located here. The shops offering discounts and shopping cards (see website) or you can check at the information center at the mall.

Galleries Lafayette

Commercial Center La Part-Dieu

Tel: 04 78 60 22 46

http://www.galerieslafayette.com/

Galleries Lafayette is world-famous for its upscale shopping and it wide range of famous brands, food stores, electronic stores and other services. The mall holds fashion shows, music festivals, movie shows as well as fashion parades. If you cannot decide what to buy use the accompanied shopping service and an expert will help you figure out how to spend your money.

Victor Hugo Street

The biggest pedestrian street in Lyon is Victor Hugo Street which is a great place to shop. The street connects Place Bellcour with Place Carnot and is located near the Peninsula quarter. Many major hotels in Lyon are located on this street. The street is crowded with restaurants, chocolate shops, gift shops, fragrance shops like Marrionaud, and clothing shops like Pied Fragile, Karboon, La City, Soho, Pamela Scott, Casual Wear and Jules (a famous brand in France).

The street is known for its selection of affordably priced shops, some of them family-run. 'La Mode a Prix Sympas' has costume jewelry at good prices, in fact you can buy a ring here for just €3. L'eau Vive it's an organic food shop that's well regarded in Lyon and which offers a large assortment of natural products. All the ingredients are held in a controlled environment and you can find useful information about raw food here.

Reserve Naturelle

http://www.reserve-naturelle.com/

If you care about your exterior health as well, the 'Natural Reservation' shop is reputable in Lyon. You can find perfumes, makeup and gifts at low prices. The products are mainly natural or with natural compounds. The prices are low, for example you can buy a natural body scrub for €1.

Bonnie & Clyde

45 Rue Haberdasher,

69002, Lyon

Tel: 04 78 38 27 55

http://bonnieetclyde.free.fr

If you are looking for shoes, Bonnie & Clyde is one of the shops you should visit. Guided by the latest European fashions, here you will find shoes designed by the greatest shoemakers from France, Italy and Spain. The quality is guaranteed and products are fairly priced varying by the material and brand.

Know Before You Go

Entry Requirements

By virtue of the Schengen agreement, visitors from other countries in the European Union will not need a visa when visiting France. Additionally Swiss visitors are also exempt. Visitors from certain other countries such as Andorra, Canada, the United Kingdom, Ireland, the Bahamas, Australia, the USA, Chile, Costa Rica, Croatia, El Salvador, Guatemala, Honduras, Israel, Malaysia, Mauritius, Monaco, Nicaragua, New Zealand, Panama, Paraguay, Saint Kitts and Nevis, San Marino, the Holy See, Seychelles, Taiwan and Japan do not need visas for a stay of less than 90 days. Visitors to France must be in possession of a valid passport that expires no sooner than three months after the intended stay. UK citizens will not need a visa to enter France. Visitors must provide proof of residence, financial support and the reason for their visit. If you wish to work or study in France, however, you will need a visa.

Health Insurance

Citizens of other EU countries are covered for emergency health care in France. UK residents, as well as visitors from Switzerland are covered by the European Health Insurance Card (EHIC), which can be applied for free of charge. Visitors from non-Schengen countries will need to show proof of private health insurance that is valid for the duration of their stay in France (that offers at least €37,500 coverage), as part of their visa application. A letter of coverage will need to be submitted to the French Embassy along with your visa application. American travellers will need to check whether their regular medical insurance covers international travel. No special vaccinations are required.

Travelling with Pets

France participates in the Pet Travel Scheme (PETS) which allows UK residents to travel with their pets without requiring quarantine upon re-entry. Certain conditions will need to be met. The animal will have to be microchipped and up to date on rabies vaccinations. In the case of dogs, France also requires vaccination against distemper. If travelling from another EU member country, you will need an EU pet passport. Regardless of the country, a Declaration of Non-Commercial Transport must be signed stating that you do not intend to sell your pet.

A popular form of travel with pets between the UK and France is via the Eurotunnel, which has special facilities for owners travelling with pets. This includes dedicated pet exercise areas and complimentary dog waste bags. Transport of a pet via this medium costs €24. The Calais Terminal has a special Pet Reception Building. Pets travelling from the USA will need to be at least 12 weeks old and up to date on rabies vaccinations. Microchipping or some form of identification tattoo will also be required. If travelling from another country, do inquire about the specific entry requirements for your pet into France and also about re-entry requirements in your own country.

Airports

There are three airports near Paris where most international visitors arrive. The largest of these is **Charles De Gaulle** (CDG) airport, which serves as an important hub for both international and domestic carriers. It is located about 30km outside Paris and is well-connected to the city's rail network. Most trans-Atlantic flights arrive here. **Orly** (ORY) is the second largest and oldest airport serving Paris. It is located 18km south of the city and is connected to several public transport options including a bus service, shuttle service and Metro rail. Most of its arrivals and departures are to other destinations within Europe. **Aéroport de Paris-Beauvais-Tillé** (BVA), which lies in Tillé near Beauvais, about 80km outside

Paris, is primarily used by Ryanair for its flights connecting Paris to Dublin, Shannon Glasgow and other cities.

There are several important regional airports. **Aéroport Nice Côte d'Azur** (NCE) is the 3rd busiest airport in France and serves as a gateway to the popular French Riviera. **Aéroport Lyon Saint-Exupéry** (LYS) lies 20km east of Lyon and serves as the main hub for connections to the French Alps and Provence. It is the 4th busiest airport of France. **Aéroport de Bordeaux** (BOD) served the region of Bordeaux. **Aéroport de Toulouse – Blagnac** (TLS), which lies 7km from Toulouse, provides access to the south-western part of France. **Aéroport de Strasbourg** (SXB), which lies 10km west of Strasbourg, served as a connection to Orly, Paris and Nice. **Aéroport de Marseille Provence** (MRS) is located in the town of Marignane, about 27km from Marseille and provides access to Provence and the French Riviera. **Aéroport Nantes Atlantique** (NTE) lies in Bouguenais, 8km from Nantes carriers and provides a gateway to the regions of Normandy and Brittany in the western part of France. **Aéroport de Lille** (LIL) is located near Lesquin and provides connections to the northern part of France.

Airlines

Air France is the national flag carrier of France and in 2003, it merged with KLM. The airline has a Flying Blue rewards program, which allows members to earn, accumulate and redeem Flying Blue Miles on any flights with Air France, KLM or any other Sky Team airline. This includes Aeroflot, Aerolineas Argentinas, AeroMexico, Air Europa, Alitalia, China Airlines, China Eastern, China Southern, Czech Airlines, Delta, Garuda Indonesia, Kenya Airways, Korean Air, Middle Eastern Airlines, Saudia, Tarom, Vietnam Airlines and Xiamen Airlines.

Air France operates several subsidiaries, including the low-cost Transavia.com France, Cityjet and Hop! It is also in partnership with Air Corsica. Other French airlines are Corsairfly and XL Airways France (formerly Star Airlines).

France's largest intercontinental airport, Charles de Gaulle serves as a hub for Air France, as well as its regional subsidiary, HOP!. It also functions as a European hub for Delta Airlines. Orly Airport, also in Paris, serves as the main hub for Air France's low cost subsidiary, Transavia, with 40 different destinations, including London, Madrid, Copenhagen, Moscow, Casablanca, Algiers, Amsterdam, Istanbul, Venice, Rome, Berlin and Athens. Aéroport de Marseille Provence (MRS) outside Marseille serves as a hub to the region for budget airlines such as EasyJet and Ryanair. Aéroport Nantes Atlantique serves as a French base for the Spanish budget airline, Volotea.

Currency

France's currency is the Euro. It is issued in notes in denominations of €500, €200, €100, €50, €20, €10 and €5. Coins are issued in €2, €1, 50c, 20c, 10c, 5c, 2c and 1c.

Banking & ATMs

If your ATM card is compatible with the MasterCard/Cirrus or Visa/Plus networks and configured for a 4-digit PIN, you will have no problem drawing money in France. Most French ATMs have an English language option. Remember to inform your bank of your travel plans before you leave. Keep an eye open around French ATMs to avoid pickpockets or scammers.

Credit Cards

Credit cards are frequently used throughout France, not just in shops, but also to pay for metro tickets, parking tickets, and motorway tolls and even to make phone calls at phone booths. MasterCard and Visa are accepted by most vendors. American Express and Diners Club are also accepted by the more tourist oriented businesses. Credit cards issued in Europe are smart cards that that are fitted with a microchip and require a PIN for each transaction. This means that a few ticket machines, self-service vendors and other businesses may not be configured to accept the older magnetic strip credit cards.

Tourist Taxes

All visitors to France pay a compulsory city tax or tourist tax ("taxe de séjour"), which is payable at your accommodation. Children are exempt from tourist tax. The rate depends on the standard of accommodation, starting with €0.75 per night for cheaper establishments going up to €4, for the priciest options. Rates are, of course, subject to change.

Reclaiming VAT

If you are not from the European Union, you can claim back VAT (or Value Added Tax) paid on your purchases in France. The VAT rate in France is 20 percent on most goods, but restaurant goods, food, transport and medicine are charged at lower rates. VAT can be claimed back on purchases of over €175 from the same shop, provided that your stay in France does not exceed six months. Look for shops that display a "Tax Free" sign. The shop assistant must fill out a form for reclaiming VAT. When you submit it at the airport, you can expect your refund to be debited within 30 to 90 days to your credit card or bank account. It can also be sent by cheque.

Tipping Policy

In French restaurants, a 15 percent service charge is added directly to your bill and itemized with the words *service compris* or "tip included". This is a legal requirement for taxation purposes. If the service was unusually good, a little extra will be appreciated. In an expensive restaurant where there is a coat check, you may add €1 per coat. In a few other situations, a tip will be appreciated. You can give an usherette in a theatre 50 cents to €1, give a porter €1 per bag for helping with your luggage or show your appreciation for a taxi driver with 5-10 percent over the fare. It is also customary to tip a hair dresser or a tour guide 10 percent.

Mobile Phones

Most EU countries, including France uses the GSM mobile service. This means that most UK phones and some US and Canadian phones and mobile devices will work in France. While you could check with your service provider about coverage before you leave, using your own service in roaming mode will involve additional costs. The alternative is to purchase a French SIM card to use during your stay in France. France has four mobile networks. They are Orange, SFR, Bouygues Telecom and Free. In France, foreigners are barred from applying for regular phone contract and the data rates are somewhat pricier on pre-paid phone services than in most European countries. You will need to show some form of identification, such as a passport when you make your purchase and it can take up to 48 hours to activate a French SIM card. If there is an Orange Boutique nearby, you can buy a SIM for €3.90. Otherwise, the Orange Holiday package is available for €39.99. Orange also sells a 4G device which enables your own portable Wi-Fi hotspot for €54.90. SFR offers a SIM card, simply known as le card for €9.99. Data rates begin at €5 for 20Mb.

Dialling Code

The international dialling code for France is +33.

Emergency Numbers

All emergencies: (by mobile) 112
Police: 17
Medical Assistance: 15
Fire and Accidents: 18
SOS All Emergencies (hearing assisted: 114)
Visa: 0800 90 11 79
MasterCard: 0800 90 13 87
American Express: 0800 83 28 20

Public Holidays

1 January: New Year's Day (Nouvel an / Jour de l'an / Premier de l'an)

March - April: Easter Monday (Lundi de Pâques)

1 May: Labor Day (Fête du Travail / Fête des Travailleurs)

8 May: Victory in Europe Day (Fête de la Victoire)

May: Ascension Day (Ascension)

May: Whit Monday (Lundi de Pentecôte)

14 July: Bastille Day (Fête nationale)

15 August: Assumption of Mary (L'Assomption de Marie)

1 November: All Saints Day (La Toussaint)

11 November: Armistace Day (Armistice de 1918)

25 December: Christmas Day (Noël)

Good Friday and St Stephens Day (26 December) are observed only in Alsace and Moselle.

Time Zone

France falls in the Central European Time Zone. This can be calculated as Greenwich Mean Time/Co-ordinated Universal Time (GMT/UTC) +2; Eastern Standard Time (North America) -6; Pacific Standard Time (North America) -9.

Daylight Savings Time

Clocks are set forward one hour on the last Sunday of March and set back one hour on the last Sunday of October for Daylight Savings Time.

School Holidays

The academic year in France is from the beginning of September to the end of June. The long summer holiday is from the beginning of July to the end of August. There are three shorter vacation periods. All schools break up for a two week break around Christmas and New Year. There are also two week breaks in February and April, but this varies per region, as French schools are divided into three zones, which take their winter and spring vacations at different times.

Driving Laws

The French drive on the ride hand side of the road. If you have a non-European driving licence, you will be able to use it in France, provided that the licence is valid and was issued in your country of residence before the date of your visa application. There are a few other provisions. The minimum driving age in France is 18. Your licence will need to be in French or alternately, you must carry a French translation of your driving permit with you.

In France, the speed limit depends on weather conditions. In dry weather, the speed limit is 130km per hour for highways, 110km per hour for 4-lane expressways and 90km per hour for 2 or 3-lane rural roads. In rainy weather, this is reduced to 110km, 100km and 80km per hour respectively. In foggy weather with poor visibility, the speed limit is 50km per hour on all roads. On urban roads, the speed limit is also 50km per hour.

By law, French drivers are obliged to carry a breathalyser in their vehicle, but these are available from most supermarkets, chemists and garages for €1. The legal limit is 0.05, but for new drivers who have had their licence for less than three years, it is 0.02. French motorways are called autorouts. It is illegal in France to use a mobile phone while driving, even if you have a headset.

Drinking Laws

The legal drinking age in France is 18. The drinking policy regarding public spaces will seem confusing to outsiders. Each municipal area imposes its own laws. In Paris, alcohol consumption is only permitted in licensed establishments. It is strictly forbidden in parks and public gardens.

Smoking Laws

From 2007, smoking has been banned in indoor spaces such as schools, government buildings, airports, offices and factories in France. The ban was extended in 2008 to hospitality venues such as restaurants, bars, cafes and casinos. French trains have been smoke free since December 2004.

Electricity

Electricity: 220-240 volts

Frequency: 50 Hz

Electricity sockets in France are unlike those of any other country. They are hermaphroditic, meaning that they come equipped with both prongs and indents. When visiting from the UK, Ireland, the USA or even another European country, you will need a special type of adaptor to accommodate this. If travelling from the USA, you will also need a converter or step-down transformer to convert the current to to 110 volts, to avoid damage to your appliances. The latest models of many laptops, camcorders, mobile phones and digital cameras are dual-voltage with a built in converter.

Food & Drink

France is a paradise for dedicated food lovers and the country has a vast variety of well-known signature dishes. These include foie gras, bouillabaisse, escargots de Bourgogne, Coq au vin, Bœuf Bourguignon, quiche Lorraine and ratatouille. A great budget option is crêpes or pancakes. Favorite sweets and pastries include éclairs, macarons, mille-feuilles, crème brûlée and croissants.

The country is home to several world-famous wine-growing regions, including Alsace, Bordeaux, Bourgogne, Champagne,

Corse, Côtes du Rhône, Languedoc-Roussillon, Loire, Provence and Sud-Ouest and correctly matching food to complimentary wine choices is practically a science. Therein lies the key to enjoying wine as the French do. It accompanies the meal. Drinking wine when it is not lunch or dinner time is sure to mark you as a foreigner. Pastis and dry vermouth are popular aperitifs and favorite after-dinner digestifs include cognac, Armagnac, calvados and eaux de vie. The most popular French beer is Kronenbourg, which originates from a brewery that dates back to 1664.

Websites

http://www.rendezvousenfrance.com/

http://www.france.com/

http://www.francethisway.com/

http://www.france-voyage.com/en/

http://www.francewanderer.com/

http://wikitravel.org/en/France

http://www.bonjourlafrance.com/index.aspx

18785088R00038

Printed in Great Britain
by Amazon